BINDED

BINDED

poems

H Warren

borealbooks

Book design by Tansica Sunkamaneevongse

Library of Congress Cataloging-in-Publication Data

Names: Warren, H., 1987– author.
Title: Binded: poems / H Warren.
Description: Pasadena: Boreal Books, [2023]
Identifiers: LCCN 2022036686 (print) | LCCN 2022036687 (ebook) | ISBN 9781597099318 (paperback) | ISBN 9781597099332 (ebook)
Subjects: LCGFT: Poetry.
Classification: LCC PS3623.A86454 B56 2023 (print) | LCC PS3623.A86454 (ebook) | DDC 811/.6—dc23/eng/20220824
LC record available at https://lccn.loc.gov/2022036686
LC ebook record available at https://lccn.loc.gov/2022036687

The National Endowment for the Arts, the Los Angeles County Arts Commission, the Ahmanson Foundation, the Dwight Stuart Youth Fund, the Max Factor Family Foundation, the Pasadena Tournament of Roses Foundation, the Pasadena Arts & Culture Commission and the City of Pasadena Cultural Affairs Division, the City of Los Angeles Department of Cultural Affairs, the Audrey & Sydney Irmas Charitable Foundation, the Meta & George Rosenberg Foundation, the Albert and Elaine Borchard Foundation, the Adams Family Foundation, Amazon Literary Partnership, the Sam Francis Foundation, and the Mara W. Breech Foundation partially support Red Hen Press.

First Edition
Published by Boreal Books
An imprint of Red Hen Press
www.borealbooks.org
www.redhen.org

ACKNOWLEDGMENTS

The most enthusiastic thank you to Peggy Shumaker for believing in my work and bringing my first full-length collection into the world!

Huge thank you to Red Hen Press and their wonderful team. I am so grateful.

I want to thank all of the editors and readers who gave many of the poems in this collection a first "home." To the following literary journals: *Iris Brown*; *Skin to Skin*; *S/tick*; *The Paper Street Journal*; *The Fem Literary Magazine*; *Pilot Light*; *Degenderettes Zine*; *SOUND Literary Magazine*; *The Bookends Review*; *The Water Stone Review*; *Anecdote Magazine*; and *Flock*.

Endless gratitude to the Rasmuson Foundation. Thank you for the funding and support through the Individual Artist Award program—this book is possible due to your continual support and validation to Alaskan artists.

Thank you to the Anchorage Museum, the University of Alaska Fairbanks, the UAF English Department and Faculty and the Death Rattle Writer's Festival crew. Big moments that shaped who I am as a writer happened in relation with these places and incredible people.

A special thank you to my friends, mentors and teachers who encouraged and inspired me: David Nikki Crouse, Sean Hill, Derick Burelson, Chris Coffman, Christine Dyer, Caitlin Scarano, Sean Enfield, Kori Hensell, Kendell Newman-Sadiik, Donald Crocker, Alyssa Quintyne, Hannah C. Hill, Rebecca Menzia, and the Harm crew.

Thank you to my sister Rebecca Schrank and brother-in-law Zachary. And a forever love and appreciation for a lifetime of support and belief in all my dreaming—to my Mom and Dad.

Lastly, a big thank you to my wife, Erin McGroarty—who feeds me and takes care of all the things while my nose is pressed to the computer screen. Thank you for all of the love and support.

CONTENTS

BINDED

CLIPPED

I forgot the way my tongue snaps in half
when men speak louder
over my own speaking

I am merely bird
limp upon a windowsill

an attempt at flying
clipped before my birth

I thought I was a boy
and cried to my mother
when I found blood between my legs

I am still her daughter
but I am not
her baby girl

BINDER

Binded

Binded breasts

Binded squished   nipple

Binded still   not flat
Binded but my nipples are hard

Binded everywhere
Binded nowhere
Binded in your stare
Binded tight

Binded tight

Binded tight   can't take off my pronoun *you* prefer
Binded rural

Binded when an older woman throws me a second glance in
        the bathroom and says   *oh*
Binded sir
Binded mam

Binded when I exchange my comfort for *your* comfort
Binded when you plead for me to wear a dress at your wedding
Binded when I refuse and I am no longer in your wedding
Binded to this barstool when he asks *how do you even fuck*
Binded when he lets me know he can *straighten me out*
Binded when she broke up with me and said *heterosexuality is easier*
Binded when I'm too afraid to take my shirt off during sex
Binded when my friends say *but you have a lot of feminine energy*

Binded when you worry about me
Binded when I worry about myself
Binded I am always a question
Binded when my mother says

stop   you are a girl

BEGIN WITH THIS

when you wake in the morning
the scent of heat
dancing   as one whole note
replays a night
never ending
movement
falling sleepless into
all the ways of sound and pulse

when a first dance
moves beyond a feeling
invasion into heart
texture of the mouth
stroke of the spine
twirling colors on the wall
soft sweeping into
the ever-rhythm of living

love is listening and laughing and asking questions
and taking party lights and music very seriously

gathered bits of song
tucked away in the north
what will sing of home

a room full of steady humming
sleeping dog
vinyl record
fat tire bikes and transparent bibs
ready for the belly of winter and patient mountains
bark stripped bleached trees
wrapped with lights in handfuls

and hand-filled walks
where the dilapidated peer
holds you safe in the pitch-black night

when you sing of home
sing about sailboat pants and where to find them
about poutine and rolling farmlands on a rickety old bus
secret shows and the enchantment of each other
the whistling tune of snow drifts
that will never break you

when you sing of home
begin with this

SEAM

(In Response to Fairbanks City Mayor's Veto of 6093
Non-Discrimination Ordinance, 2019)

don't clip into my stitching

please understand
I sewed myself together

from a wound soaked in fabric
with pretty patterns

when I came out
to my mother
a wedding dress
became un-useful

when I came out
to my city
my tears became
militant
my body
the topic
of debate
of
    seam

fem butch ripping into pieces of cloth
I am wearing 6-0-9-3 for everyone to see
for everyone to see   me
I
strip
down

and I sew myself together
again   I sew myself together
again   I sew myself together
again   I sew myself back together

I sew myself an outfit of
vulnerability

through vulnerability we feel fear

through vulnerability we speak to pain

but   through vulnerability we find connection

and joy

and love

so I'm going to have a whole wardrobe full of vulnerability

I'm going to feel so polished in these shoes I walk in

thanks to all of you
I feel so much love
in the fitting
of our hands interlocked

our community

our gentle seamstress

POST-ELECTION 2016

I feel her next to me   awake
with the warmth of her breath against my neck
I am not shaken by the whispers of uncertainty

our bodies   bent
become
riot

in the bed of our blush
in the bed of our stones
our shape
our
    smolder

AT WAR WITH MYSELF

dress me
baggy covered
missing breasts

when you say
handsome
I speak
awful femininity

tell me
about my
burning body
in a schoolyard

undress me
halfway
under
darkness

please look away

WHAT WE DON'T TALK ABOUT
MAY HARM YOU

she writes a list of her horrors and titles it God
or whatever God names her in the night
black latches like shadow puppets
against the bedroom
walls   she asks me
if there are words for her hurt
when her hurt from years before
become what is hurting now

she tells me she is split
into one hundred fifty parts
she says the floor is cold
it feels like concrete
her speak like weighted keys of a piano
underneath a child's fingers

the ways in which our bodies remember
remembering
what we lock away is
time travel

is the measure of

the measure of   loss
is   a spectacle
is a hot moon hung to quiver between
the curve of a palm pressed against the teeth   is
a hunger for   starvation
for feeding on an answer that has no language

A CHILD   A SEPARATE MOUTH

my hands will make a tower of dead grass
and crush the ants that climb the hill   before
I spit the chipped ends of my coral teeth
out for you   a keepsake   remember me
I will split your lips apart and sign our
palms with the blood of your tongue   with my tongue
a prayer   rotten   bruised like apple skin
I will think about the way a fist can
bruise the bone like wine stains carpet red like
vibrations from my mouth when I'm at home
with no one else at home to hear the dog
howl moon howl hard whispers in the darkness

you ghost   how I howl as you   approach me

MY FIRST CHEST BINDER

tuck each breast
into tightness
the difficult
of breath

I inherited
my first binder

handed down
by one
of the only two
trans men
I know
in this rural
Alaskan town

what was worn before
I said my name
to check
if it still fit?

from a side angle
my chest looks lumpy
and deformed
the opposite effect
as if I'm stuffing a bra

if I suffocate
in this
compression
call it
a life well spent

ANTI-BATHROOM BILL:
A POEM WITH P

a particular phobic
specific
transphobic
persons placing
displacing
my person
my people
just people
all human
online posting
and posting
warning
there's crossdressers in the bathroom
please tell
the children:

watch out
for
pedophiles

peeing perpendicular
hands clasped
in prayer

it's God's aim

that pee is
a privilege

P is for perverts
prying open the bathroom stall
in a panic

about what my genitals say
or don't say
about me

P is for pacification
peacekeeping in perpetual
process of oppression
appeasing the loudest bigot in his pew

midstream
a stranger
stops me from urinating
misplaced
pain
mistaking
the pulpit
for the toilet

P is for paraphrase
praising psalms
picked precise
purposed
for powerful protestations
interpreting a straight and
special selection
for appropriate
places for piss
and scripture

please

just let me pee
in peace

pretend that my short hair is just a hair cut

prepare for people using the bathroom for particular activities like   peeing

prevent the impulse to pry open any bathroom stalls to *just make sure*

practice good hygiene and wash your hands thoroughly

and please

if you propose an anti-bathroom bill
propping up pillars and platforms for hate

piss off

GROWING

I bought a plant

a mature orchid with violet petals

I counted thirteen flowers
looking ready to topple sideways
I'm unsure of what I know about growing

I lied to the garden worker at Lowe's

I said *I'll take good care of it*
she said *you are taking my favorite*

this is the first plant
I have ever claimed
for my own

I love each bloom for its impermanence
then   the smell of wilt
reminding me
of what I should
                    let go

WHEN I SAW HER CORPSE

as if   I saw   lightning strike the other end of my office desk
the alarms rang   and I knew it was not   a fire drill
I knew she was not dead   yet

I knew she was not dead   but   when I saw her corpse
flatten to the floor   curl the legs of my office desk like an abandoned animal
I took the shortcut past my nerves

                          reached out with my hands

those pleading eyes   glossy

                                    when I tried to put those lids to rest   I saw
                                          my own eyes
                                          looking at my own
                                          body detached from my own
                                          body hovering down
                                          looking   above

there!   look!

a silver button rests upon the bottom step of a concrete stairwell

the color of the button changes with the color of the day and today
when I saw her corpse scab a white scar over those bells
shrieking   *lock it down*
                    lock it down
                                    I knew

TWO TYPES OF SMILE

for every sir and mam
is an open sky
thundering hail

I am so bored of the sky

I cringe at its every mention

always the sky
looking soft
pastel purple
looking perfect
mistaken
as normal

what did the sky ever do
but hold a body in place
in limitations
and pressure
talk about the weather

there's a storm on the way

I am smiling

not a single cloud

I am smiling

how can I help you sir?
how can I help you mam?
I am smiling

NAME ME WHAT YOU WILL

her soils
from a bottle full of cut teeth
grew seeds

her shells
chewed and spit
into bottles full of ocean

her salt
lingers along the skin
that flakes

THE OCCUPATIONAL HAZARD
OF LIVING YOUR TRUTH

watch what happens to the outspoken
the doors open
and the vulgar come marching
one beat of the drum
at the same time
friends evaporate
like an echo

what is first   a boundary
becomes
a fork-shaped road
from my mouth
    a crossing of ghosts

what is once tender
burns
when left
unattended

MOTHER'S DAY

(in conversation with Lucille Clifton & dedicated to my Mom)

when the shadows
follow me home
I listen
beyond the stillness
I can hear her
whisper
among the leaves
what has made you strong

a sensitive skin
unconditional birth

warm moon
round face

the tan of the sky
a lineage
of
fire

GET BACK TO WORK AMERICA

fellow community members
the recession is coming

get back to work

make it great again

absent from a press conference
the image of the dead

what Covid swallowed

the men with guns
safe at the capitol

like a grenade
discomfort
explodes into
oppression

it's all revenue

there's a formula for this

priority issues
will include
whiteness

national lenders
bent language

look at the language

the institution
of the PPE
and the coffin

industry is
a level playing field
for the hostage

remember
there are more important things
than living
swab down the throat
open the doors
get with the program
get back to work

buzzword
rhetoric
disaster

this is a pandemic
after all

have you considered
applying for
prayer and well wishes?

AN HONEST BUDGET

by Michael J Dunleavy

includes

five guiding principles: ONE

> *- expenditures cannot exceed existing revenue*
> *-TWO the budget is built on core functions that impact a majority of Alaskans*
> *-THREE maintain and protect our reserves*
> *-FOUR the budget does NOT TAKE additional funds from Alaskans*
> *   through taxes or the   PFD*
> *-FIVE it must be sustainable   predictable   affordable*

> *sustainable   predictable   affordable*

> *sustainable   predictable   affordable*

The Faces That You Cut

The Faces That You Cut

The Faces That You Cut

expenditures cannot exceed existing revenue

The Faces That You Cut

> expenditures cannot consider the existing
> > the living
> > the breathing
> > the homeless
> > the hungry

                                        our elders
                                        the hurt

                                        the hurt

The Faces That You Cut
the budget is built on core functions
that impact the majority of Alaskans

The Faces That You Cut
the budget is built to break our core functions
the budget doesn't care
about morality
an honest budget is not
an honest function for

                                        the living
                                        the breathing
                                        the homeless
                                        the hungry
                                        our elders
                                        the hurt

                                        the hurt

The Faces That You Cut
maintain and protect our reserves

The Faces That You Cut
maintain and protect
your reserves
of oil
also death
and active colonization

The Faces That You Cut
maintain and protect
yourself
and no one else
and certainly not

                              the homeless
                              the hungry
                              our elders
                              the hurt

                              the hurt

The Faces That You Cut
the budget does not take additional funds from Alaskans through
    taxes or the PFD

The Faces That You Cut
the budget does not take
a bootstrap
a holster
or muscles of exceptionalism
isms are not welcomed so do not try
any honesty here in the wild wild west
because calling this divisive is in and of itself
divisive

cuts are rational didn't you know
we rent planes and fly to the gates of the Arctic
and fuck up the earth
and the people
and our elders
and the hurt

the hurt

sustainable   predictable   affordable
sustainable   predictable   affordable
sustainable   predictable   affordable

OBEDIENCE   A RITUAL

you are four years old   your father hands you a brick   he says *this is
  lighter than it feels*

you are in a garage   the walls are cluttered with newspaper   photos
  of aftermaths   rusted
tools hang from the ceiling the concrete floor is splattered with grease
  your father grunts
against a band saw   sawdust floats into your breath

you drop the brick while you are testing its lightness

you stare at the blood   you stare at your separation

your toenail ripped off   the flesh underneath is hot pink

you can't remember if you cried

your father begins sanding wood

FREESTONE: "A FRUIT HAVING A STONE TO WHICH THE FLESH DOES NOT CLING"

It is not the season
I am not an orchard

I find brutal men
blossom
when bitten

this is not a peach
a painted still life
or a symbol
for your tongue to interpret

I did not ask
for a foot rub

I am not your flower

I am not your rotten fable

BLINKING IN KNOTS

I've handcuffed myself again   to an open sea
act like you know
lungs underwater   my scratchy throat   a tightrope act

I hear the sky is a menace   I watch the clouds slither

eyesight in smoke   my cut felt stomach   scrape and tar

I know what the moon can give
and I know what she can break

a twisted wrist   the blindness of teeth   my knees   the give

act like you know
the black of a burnt structure
a split stone along the road
the moan of a dying animal

act like you know the way metal melts
the way a bloody lip tastes
the way any bruise can find   excuse

what I know is the knockout and the dying fall
caught by the dust-lit corners of a concrete wall
the nickel sent knuckled slump of a back hand

                and a rippled spat apology

BUYING CLOTHES

button unbutton

button unbutton

bone bruises I don't know about
an aching
blossoms from my chest

shirt won't button at my chest
shirt unbuttons at my chest

what size is
my identity

the measurement of
looking too fem
looking too butch
reminds me of a safety pin
unable to clasp
two forms
of being

WHY I DIDN'T REPORT

my body was not ready
to remember
what my body remembers
are cut fingernail bits bit from my teeth
that sprinkle the kitchen table is a gray card table or a wooden table
maybe
there was no table
I sat and I chewed off my fingers because without hands
my body can't feel
what's around me
my body has no excuse
if I have no fingers
to grip around the hands around my throat
maybe
I have no throat
maybe I lost my excuses somewhere back in the dark alley I've never
    walked
maybe there were no hands
only a ripped off button a tan button a silver button
an emergency button I didn't have to push for help
I didn't remember my body
about my body
about an invisible wound
I don't remember

WHAT WOUNDS BECOME

(in conversation with Torrin A Greathouse)

a ghost still living

a ghost still living   living still   a ghost   drones
from the drain of my mouth from the drain of my mouth
          from my mouth
ghosts

still living   in the noise
of a new vocabulary

my mouth still speaking
a still
vocabulary
much like drones

what becomes
of a ghost still living

in the noise of my vocabulary

in my body
boy
in my body
girl
in my body
ghost

URGENT

for what you call
the mutilation of my body

all I am asking for
is a flat chest

and for you to call me boy
once in a while

HYPERVIGILANCE

tuck a dust-covered bra
in the corner
of a shed

keep it locked

I am at capacity

for the grotesque
names are born

freak
fag
dyke

there is home somewhere
that blinks its eyelash
with welcoming arms

PRODUCED UNDER CONDITIONS
OF INTENSE HEAT

is a daughter dancing
waves away
with kitchen spoons
wilted blooms
blue the underbelly
of her eyes

she dances
upon shards
of glass

cuts between
her toes
suggest
her surrender
to a house
full of wolves

she finds her son
dead in a plastic bag
she finds her mother
crying behind the shadow
of a lampshade
unnoticed   the dog
eats dinner
dribbles bits
onto the carpet

when he stumbles home
she will play scarecrow coffin

when he rattles doorframes
she will pinch back onion downpour

backhand combos
quick jab when he

she will
cry
blackbird

RICKETS

I've lined my throat
with words I don't know

in the clutch
of stillness
between
a dim sculpted bruise
and ground
I shake

I sound
off the wail of rotted color
watch as the blue burns
not like sky
and not like rain

this is not

           a rape

BORN TO MAKE YOU HAPPY

for Amara

I am a child from the glass half empty
do you remember
your drink
as a blessing

will you
bless my grown-up body
as your own
body
drenched in fragrance
small girls use
to smell grown up faster

small girl
grew up without
knowing the soothe
or calm
of jasmine

she asks about the blue lotus
where it can be found

MINUTES TO MORNING

time to use compassion
as a shield
wake up
another day

that indent in the pillow
that cushions my head
from both sides

the comforter
keeps an entire night
of body warmth

seems like
the only safe place to be

too many people don't have that

WHAT DO YOU SAY WHEN DOGS DIE

for Portia

the curl of a good boy
                                    the best boy
still rests against the knees

ghost strokes
nothing there

if only
we had one more year
for every porcupine quill
plucked from your mouth

to run
carefree
along moonlit trails

to lay in the tall grass
by the river
mourning
together
the unexpected

gathering the buried
forgotten
in the yard
how will we calm
the howl
of friends lost

OIL AND ICE

(Reworking Robert Frost)

some say the world will end in fire
some worlds with ICE
ending now

the taste of desire
dipped in oil
trumps
the taste of   clean water
the smell of   overcrowded cages
the sight of   children   separated
unable to hear
their mothers

we know enough of hate

we know enough of hate

from those who favor ICE
from those who favor oil
destruction made
great again
twice over with no suffice

BETWEEN A ROCK AND A ROCK
IS THE DISTANCE SPENT SEARCHING
FOR FERTILE SOIL

when she smiles
I try to catch her teeth
with my eyes closed

what animates my skin
so flushed

there are men
like shadows
passing through
our chests
pressing spears
against our skulls
carving DYKE
into our skins

ALL THE WAYS IN WHICH WE HURT

all the ways in which we hurt
revealed
in webs
of power dynamics

each thread
holds in place
the delicate
or the dead

RIVER BABIES

(in conversation with Toni Morrison)

troubled mothers   darkness does not leave this place
there are babies drowning in rivers with only few swimmers
with only few arms to wrap around few babies   there are babies
that will drown

it is   *a hot*   *hot*   *thing*

there are babies that will drown with only few swimmers   the river is an
     overflow   of lost children with no mothers and no fathers   and if these
     children have mothers and fathers
then they are left to fend for themselves

there are fathers who beat mothers and those mothers beat themselves   and each
     father who thinks he owns   a beaten mother is   a baby in the river   and
each mother who cannot leave   a beater father whether she wants to or doesn't
     want to is   a baby   in the river

there is a current in the mind that the swimmer must follow
there is a current in the body that the swimmer must follow
there is a current in sex   that the swimmer must follow
before the swimmer can swim and help a baby rescue their own selves

there is only so far that a swimmer can swim

it is   *a hot*   *hot*   *thing*

EMERGING

I am only emerging
from the old ways
of knowing myself

if ever could I know myself

the gift of language
is a continual discovery of
myself

how long it took me to know
there are no rules
in being
myself

take the plunge
invent new words
invent new tools
and build myself

WHAT WILL I NAME MYSELF

imagining myself
as a girl
again and again

imagining myself
as a boy
again and again

I imagine
all of this imagining
will define me

FIRST COMMUNION

stained glass church windows

a short hymn echoes
beyond the coda

the holy spirit
in our knees

candlewax
clumps in my hair

a young girl
white dress
learning dissociation

isn't this the way of baptism?

the first time
I asked the Lord
for a penis

the first time
he said
yes

then
sunday school
confused me
of my place in this world

YOUR RESISTANCE TO MY TRANSITION

I cannot give you an image
when I do not have an image for myself

I would show you my body
but I am told to love my body
for what it is

how can we have a conversation
if you do not want a conversation

how can I give you an image
when you have given me an image
of your own

when I tell you I am transitioning
what I mean is
I am always in transition

when I give you my language
I was hoping you would listen

I cannot give you an image
when I do not have an image for myself
when you have given me an image of your own

THE STIGMA OF SURVIVING
QUEER VIOLENCE

she follows my wreckage
                        with *you*
could splinter anything

my stomach
a croon and clawed out throat of a gut

listen to the crack of my tongue

I spit a shade of yolk film
at the curse of her feet

split the shell around my eyes
and I will say   *thank you*

let's assume I am the dog act
of her folly   turned   pet
where my knees
are the only part of my body
worth bending

I am so skeletal
against the gray
walls of our apartment
where my head just hit

WELLNESS CHECK

it's hard to see you
dear   a death
along the roadside
littered beer cans
around an open gut

I am speeding past you to the next town

MOTHER CARRIES WHAT HER MOTHER CARRIED FROM A BOTTLE FULL OF CUT TEETH

I will lock the hurt into itself

I will read a book

I will bathe my body
I will take a walk

I will force a meal down into my empty gut

I will learn to sew a patch over the holes of my skin
I will listen to my silence

I will sleep for only a dream of reckless time
I will try to love a stranger I don't even know
I will brush my teeth so I can taste clean
I will learn to bake bread so I can watch life rise

I will drink more water

I will watch my hands like a mindless movie
I will color a prayer orange of a sky settling its rage
I will only speak with intention

I want to save the dog from its dying howl

DYSPHORIA

in the dark
I forget I have breasts

but you said
yes

you said
my nipples are imaginary

like the body is

only defined elsewhere

I am not defined
cut or rugged
when the lights turn on

I see myself
only as imaginary

SKIPPING OVER NEWS HEADLINES
THAT START WITH TRANS

soul attack

disconnected
blink
red
skin
dehydrates
the power of positivity
is privilege

head aches
autopilot
daydream
collapse

a facial twitch
develops

hides
under bedsheets

rapid pulse
attitude
stuck
in the cycle
of groan

I thought I would have fought
a strong argument
for my existence

somewhere at the intersect
of extinguished fire

wood left to smolder
overnight

GRABBED IN A BATHROOM

as woman
I knew hypervigilance

as nonbinary
I know it even more

my eyes
on the floor
breathing
stale shit
that lingers

dart quick
into a stall

the echo of judgement
a deafening stream of water
as if all the sinks are running hot

the steam of it all
blurs the image of me

BREAK UP

is it the soft
of my voice
deserving of burial

I kill the feminine part of me
for my lovers
who want men

the swallowed
oval scream
when I watch
her leave

a reminder that
I am not invited
to the exclusive club
of the stained glass
church house
or
spiritual normativity

my lover throws my blouse
in the trash
replaces it with a baggy
button up

this is when I learn
existing between two points
of gender
is unknown

THE SUBJECT OF BREASTS

this will remain unspoken

choked back impulse
or a lecture or a fight

did you hear about the trans woman
they found in the dumpster
that is what a friend says
about the subject
of breasts

what blossoms
from my chest

only words
no one wants to hear

watch what happens
to the outspoken

there's no setting boundaries
without living radical

haven't I spent my whole life
living on my own terms?

COURTSIDE REVIEW

sweat leather drips
through the net
swish my wrist
bent
arm raised
on the back jog

behind the back
moves feel
feelings

reverse shake
breaks aching
ankles in the run

I love this game

I'm setting the scene

I'm not too short
for the paint
and the box out
fills the gym
with heart
beating away
everything but
ball

6:00 a.m. I'm up

9:00 p.m. I'm up

on the jump
falling into seven

concussions

brains
on the court
I *was* smart
about my body

elbows out
shoulders dipped
padded knees
and a fifty-foot peripheral
was safety
was awareness
was a confident stance
in the face of any loss

what the score board tells
is final

when the clock runs out

what the score board tells
is fuel

for the next game
and the game after

I'm setting the weight
the heavy lifting

it takes
to win

then he says
put your feet on my lap

then he says
don't tell anyone

DISPATCH FROM ALASKA

while you binge watch Netflix
with a bowl of ice cream

some of us are taking care
of our borderline neighbors

as sexual predators
continue to dominate
the discourse

the pandemic hit
long before
the privileged
felt fear

we go to work
wonder
if anyone will die
in the soup kitchen
this morning

maybe the true pandemic
is that we assume
the toilet paper
absent from the shelves
is selfish
that we forget to hold space
for those struggling with mental health
of anxiety
of all the ways in which
we are unique
in processing fear

maybe the true pandemic
is the loss
of a compassionate lens
that capitalism made us this way

maybe the true pandemic
is that the Indigenous of Alaska
have been dying for years
no one gave a fuck

maybe the true pandemic
is the way we laugh
when told to *just*
call our doctor
if we feel symptoms

maybe the true pandemic
is forgetting that
our neighbors
on the streets
deserved a space
to self-quarantine
a long time ago

A LOVE SONG

let us go then
beyond our wind-blown lips
our stuttering fists clenched tight around whatever is around   I
think there's sound   still   in the bones of our future   could you
mutter me a sweet rebirth take me in like   hunger   like
gravitation   pull me down

                                    pull me   down

                                                pull me   I'm   hot ash
swept along the floorboards   your forehead   red for my
gasp and blaze my   accelerated plunder full of spine   my
vanishing hands stopping short of a tender bruise and blush
bright lick the dust from the corners of our   blue   hour
levitate a torch   a tongue   downward   hipbone orbit stream

our bodies bent
in riot

our bodies bent
in riot

BIOGRAPHICAL NOTE

H Warren (they/them) is a poet and musician from Fairbanks, Alaska. They received their MFA in creative writing and poetry from the University of Alaska Fairbanks and are currently an MSW candidate with the University of New England online. H is a 2019 Rasmuson Individual Artist Award recipient.